Broken but not Bound

Poems of Healing and Deliverance

Written by Michelle Stadard

Illustrations by Terrance McDow and Omani J. Stadard

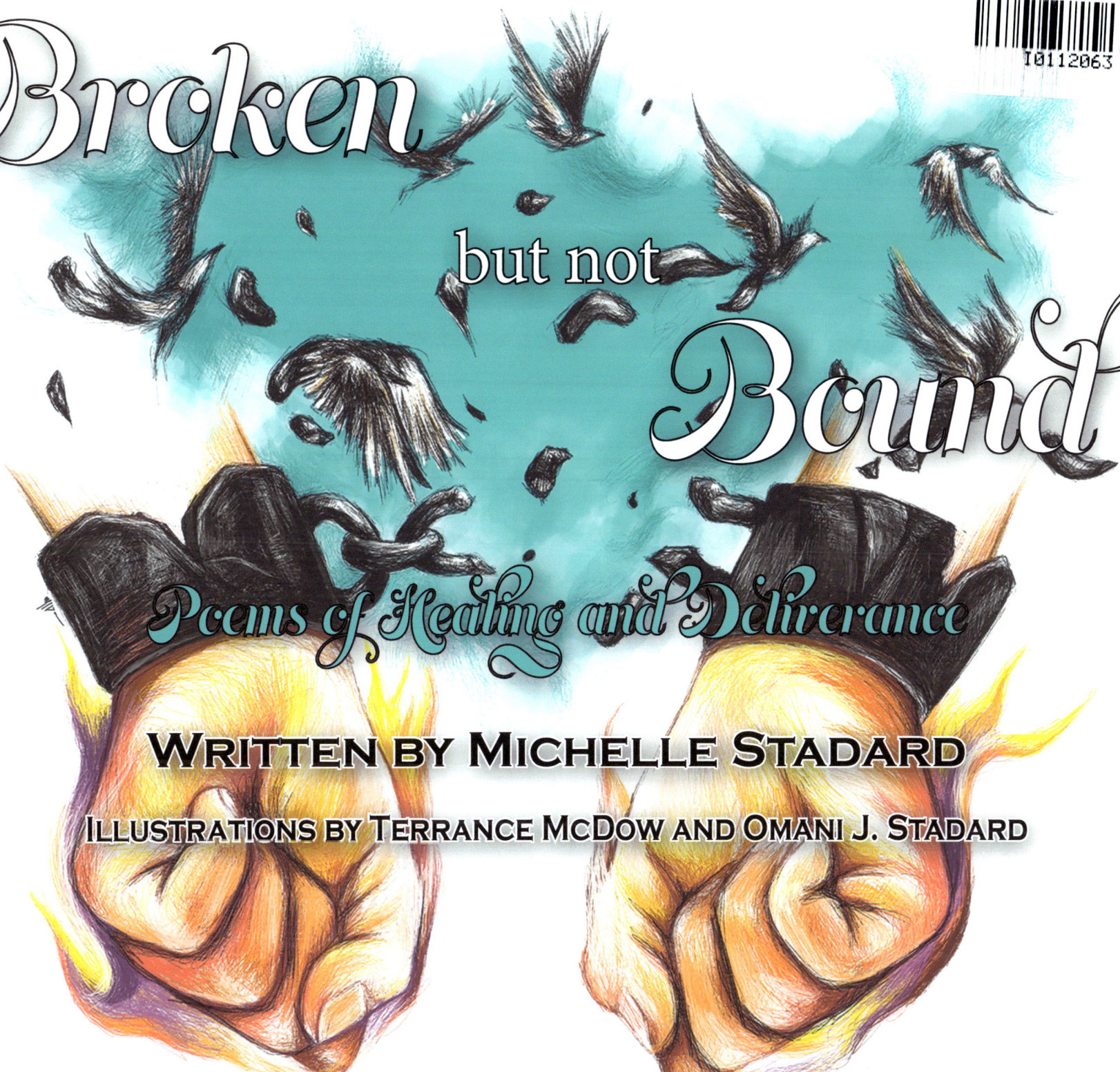

Illustrations by Omani Stadard grace pages 11, 13, 19, 35 and 47.

Illustrations by Terrance McDow grace the cover and title page and pages 7, 16, 22, 25, 28, 31, 37, 40, 43 and 45.

Published by:

McDougal & Associates

18896 Greenwell Springs Road

Greenwell Springs, LA 70739

www.ThePublishedWord.com

McDougal & Associates is an organization dedicated to spreading the Gospel of the Lord Jesus Christ to as many people as possible in the shortest time possible.

ISBN:

978-1-950398-16-4 Trade Paper Version

978-1-950398-17-1 Hardback Version

Printed On Demand

For Worldwide Distribution

Acknowledgments

I would like to thank God who is the head of my life and my All. I thank Him for giving me this gift, for without Him nothing that I do is possible.

I would like to thank my publishers, the McDougals, Harold and Andrea. I thank God for giving you the vision and being a blessing in making this book a reality.

I would also like to thank my husband and children for always being there for me.

A special thank-you goes out to my son, Omani Stadard. I'm proud of all your hard work in helping me with the illustrations for this book.

A shout-out to Terrance McDow for the amazing gift of art God has bestowed in your hands. Thank you for blessing me by helping with the illustrations.

I would also like to thank friends and family for their support, whether in word or deed. Please know that you are loved and appreciated.

Contents

Introduction

When you're broken, many times it seems that the pain will never end. It may look like there is no hope, no light at the end of the tunnel. But God gives us hope in His Word so that we can rest on His promises. He has promised that He will give us strength when we have none of our own and that He will never leave us nor forsake us (see Deuteronomy 31:6). Many times, when we're broken, we seem to have lost our focus or our sight of Him, because of all the hurt and pain we've had to endure. But it is in our brokenness that God, the Divine Potter, molds us into the vessel He has destined us to be.

In our brokenness, our spirits are humbled, and we become more like Jesus. Then He teaches us to keep our eyes on Him and on the things of God, not on the pains of our past. He teaches us to hold on to His Word and to have faith in Him and His promises. He teaches us to forgive and to let go. It is when we let go that He is able to free us, and we can then allow Him to assume the navigation of our lives. He is more than able to bring to pass all that concerns you and me.

In the midst of our trials and storms, we seem to listen to and hold on to every other voice but God's. But it is when we are attuned to *His* voice that He can guide us through all the storms and trials and on to victory. He returns to us the strength we seem to have lost in the fight.

Many things that we have faced still have us bound in our spirits, but God is our Strength and our Deliverer. When we are weakened on the battled field, as warriors of God, we tend to become fearful, but God ensures us in His Word that He is with us every moment. He has not given us a spirit of fear, but of power, and love and a sound mind (see 2 Timothy 1:7). Now the Holy Spirit guides us, and we can speak to every storm and come forth from it courageous and victorious. Christ has freed us from everything that comes to keep us stuck or stagnated.

These are the themes I have struck in the following writings. I experienced it all, and He was there to lighten my pathway. Let us now keep our eyes on Jesus. We can trust Him to guide us.

Michelle Stadard

Introduction to Broken But Not Bound

Broken—"crushed, exhausted, depressed and oppressed"
Bound—"a limitation or restriction, tied to something that limits confines or restrains us"

The state of brokenness ... It's temporary and only a set-up for your deliverance, for where God wants to take you and use you. Run to Jesus and let Him completely heal you by setting you free. We, as believers, can be bound by many things that cause us to have relationship issues with our God. Many times, we can be bound spiritually. But God is our Savior, Healer and Deliverer, and He wants us not to be trapped or tied to anything but Him.

Broken But Not Bound

I've been broken but not bound. I've been cast down but not forgotten. God says that the chains of my captivity are loosed and my faith in Him was the key to my freedom. He said, "Arise, my child. I have need of thee. So, be healed and delivered. I spoke the Word and depression had to leave." The thoughts of contemplating suicide you wouldn't believe, but God told me, "You shall live and not die. You will not abort this time this precious spiritual seed conceived inside of you. You will survive and, of course, there will be glorying in the aftermath."

I've been broken but not bound. I've struggled with low self-esteem because I really didn't believe in *me*. Then, God whispered and told me that I was beautiful. He had wonderfully created me with uniqueness and in His image. Now, He said, "Run on, my child, and be free."

I've been broken but not bound. I've had daddy issues. My father and I never really saw eye to eye on anything. I suffered from the brokenness of not having a good relationship with him, which caused me to plant a bitter seed within. Carrying that seed definitely got me nowhere, so forgiving my father aided my spiritual growth. God told me, "Wipe your tears and always remember that I love you. I'm your Daddy times two. Release him and move forward because carrying unnecessary weight only stunts your growth."

I've been broken but not bound. I had to deal with family generational curses of sexual abuse, family members not being able to control themselves and keep their hands to themselves, so they were where they didn't belong, and that was all over me. I was scared to tell anyone because of my age. Who is ever going to believe you when you're so young. "Shut your mouth!" So the joke's on you. God says, "I allowed you to experience this hurt, for I was one hundred percent God and man. I, too, had to bear a cross during My time on earth. I have been broken and crushed, but your salvation was well worth all My pain."

Introduction to Arise

Many times, as believers, we get distracted and caught up in what's going on around us and begin to lose focus on God and the plan He has for our lives. God wants our focus to be completely on Him, and the work He has for us to do. He wants us to arise and take a stand for Him. He is calling us, His people, to do the work and complete the assignments He has called us to do. Too many times we let doubt and fears settle in. God says in His Word *"For God hath not given us the spirit of fear; but of power, and of love, and of a sound mind"* (2 Timothy 1:7). God has already qualified and equipped us with what we need to do His work. Now He wants us to arise from disappointments, minor setbacks, negativity, and all of the hurts and pains from our past. He wants us to arise from excuses, like "I can't do it" when He said in His Word, *"I can do all things through Christ which strengtheneth me"* (Philippians 4:13). He wants us to arise and take a stand for His Gospel, which is the "Good News." He wants us to share His message with everybody we come in contact with. Let us arise and take a stand, by doing the will of God.

Arise

Arise, mighty warring soldiers of God. The time is now. We must rise up to take our places and rightfully claim what God deemed belongs to us. The enemy thought he had stolen your joy, so you got distracted and complacent and stopped pushing and praising. As they say nowadays, you just "fell off." You couldn't make up your mind, so you didn't finish the assignment.

You were too blind to even realize that it was crucial, and the anointing bursting on the inside of you was truly valuable, for you were carrying purpose. The result was that the baby was aborted. It wasn't birthed out full term, so it came out a stillborn, and all because you didn't have the patience or the heart of the worshiper God was developing in you. Haven't you read in the book of Proverbs that patience is needed, for it is a virtue, and true soldiers need it, for it is a fruit of the Spirit, and it completes and perfects godliness within you?

"Arise," God says. "No more abortions!" Now pay attention and keep focused. Instead, you wanted to serve two masters. As the songwriter once wrote, you wanted the best of both worlds because one just didn't satisfy you. You can't have it your way. Life isn't a Burger King. Get a grip! You can't please God by trying to walk in the Spirit as well as the natural. He has given you specific instructions to let go of everything that's not like or becoming of Him. He said to walk after Him with all of your heart and truly mean it.

"Arise!" God says. "Not by might or power, but by My Spirit. You've already won and have the victory, for you are My chosen vessel. You can't see it because it's not tangible. But haven't you read in the Word of God that *Faith is the substance of things hoped for, the evidence of things not seen.'* Arise," God says. "How are you going to preach or attempt to speak a word over somebody talking about deliverance, but the Deliverer is telling you that the same word you're speaking is for you, and you need to really believe it."

Arise! God is tired of all your excuses. You come up with every reason as to why God shouldn't use you. So you stopped pushing for that season. Oh, and the one you tried about your battle equipment not properly fitting you …. God is sick of it. So you figured you'll give it up, for you didn't even feel worthy to wear the uniform. God says to you, "Arise! I am almighty, for I know all things. I've called and ordained you from your mother's womb."

"Arise! You are worthy! My ways are not your ways. Suit up, for these are trying times, the last and evil days. I need you to be Kingdom minded. I've already prepared you, mighty warrior, for spiritual warfare. Arise!" God says. "You are worthy. I have deemed it so from the beginning, for I am the preeminent One—even before I spoke."

Introduction To Hinds' Feet

On this spiritual journey, there are many levels, and God is trying to get us through every one of them. He wants us to focus by seeking Him in daily communion, prayer and fasting. Every level is not the same. With the different levels, you run into different territory and terrains. Many of us are afraid of the new and change, but change is necessary for you to advance in Christ. Many times we become stuck and complacent with the familiar, what we know, but God is trying to tell us to get out of the familiar, what we know, and be introduced to the unfamiliar. He wants us to trust that He will take us through the many different levels in Him.

Having hinds' feet will help encourage you not to give up but to hang in there. With God-given hinds' feet, you can face trials and tribulations with joy, for God has given you the strength to hurdle (with hinds' feet) over them and the courage to stand high on top of mountains. Let God continue to promote and elevate you to the next dimensions in Him.

Hinds' Feet

God has given me hinds' feet, not to walk about, but to leap triumphantly with joy over all of my troubles. Listen, God didn't say we wouldn't have problems, but He has given us strength to conquer all of what seem to be the toughest obstacles. It may seem as though all Hell is surrounding me. I will continue to praise God and rejoice, you see, for my strength is in Him and faith is my key, for He has given me the feet of the deer.

Hinds' feet … He said, the feet of the deer, to hurdle over every trail. He has equipped me to stand high with hinds' feet on the peak of the mountaintops. In God, there's only room for love, and fear doesn't even exists. With confidence, I will not just walk but gallop elegantly with grace, carefree, because with hinds' feet He's allowed me to defeat the enemy by overcoming my trials with ease. The joy of the Lord I've sought is always in front of me. My comfort is in Jesus Christ, and His Word assures me that His peace surpasses all of man's understanding.

Hinds' feet God has given me. You see, the enemy didn't win. Satan thought he had annihilated me and got the best of me, but it was only a test. God says, "I'm taking you higher, for you've graduated and need hinds' feet to complete your advance and excel through the next levels." God told me that only with your eyes will you look and see the destruction of the wicked. The righteous, yes, the ones who do right in His sight, are safe. In this journey, there's only one way, and it is up. And, yes, the just and only the just shall live by faith.

Are you ready for the next levels?

Yet I will rejoice in the LORD, I will joy in the God of my salvation. The LORD God is my strength, and he will make my feet like hinds' feet, and he will make me to walk upon mine high places. — Habakkuk 3:18-19

Introduction to the Face of Love

The face of love is about God's love expressed to His children in the highest way. God sent His only Son to take upon Himself the sins of the whole world. God wants us to express this same love every day in the way we interact with one another.

I know that many times we feel that it is extremely hard to love, for someone has wronged us or (the other way around) we have wronged someone and just don't know how to approach or fix the situation. When we allow God to lead us and pray for forgiveness, He helps us by making those rightful decisions to love His way. He gave us instructions in His Word. He wants us to love one another the way He loves us.

God's love is not based upon conditions. He doesn't have rules or limits, nor does He choose whom He loves, for He is unconditional and without limits. God's love is limitless and everlasting. He loves everyone the same and equally regardless of our past and faults. The only way we are able to love Him and others is through the indwelling of His Holy Spirit. We truly know that the love of God abides in us when we allow Him to teach us how to love.

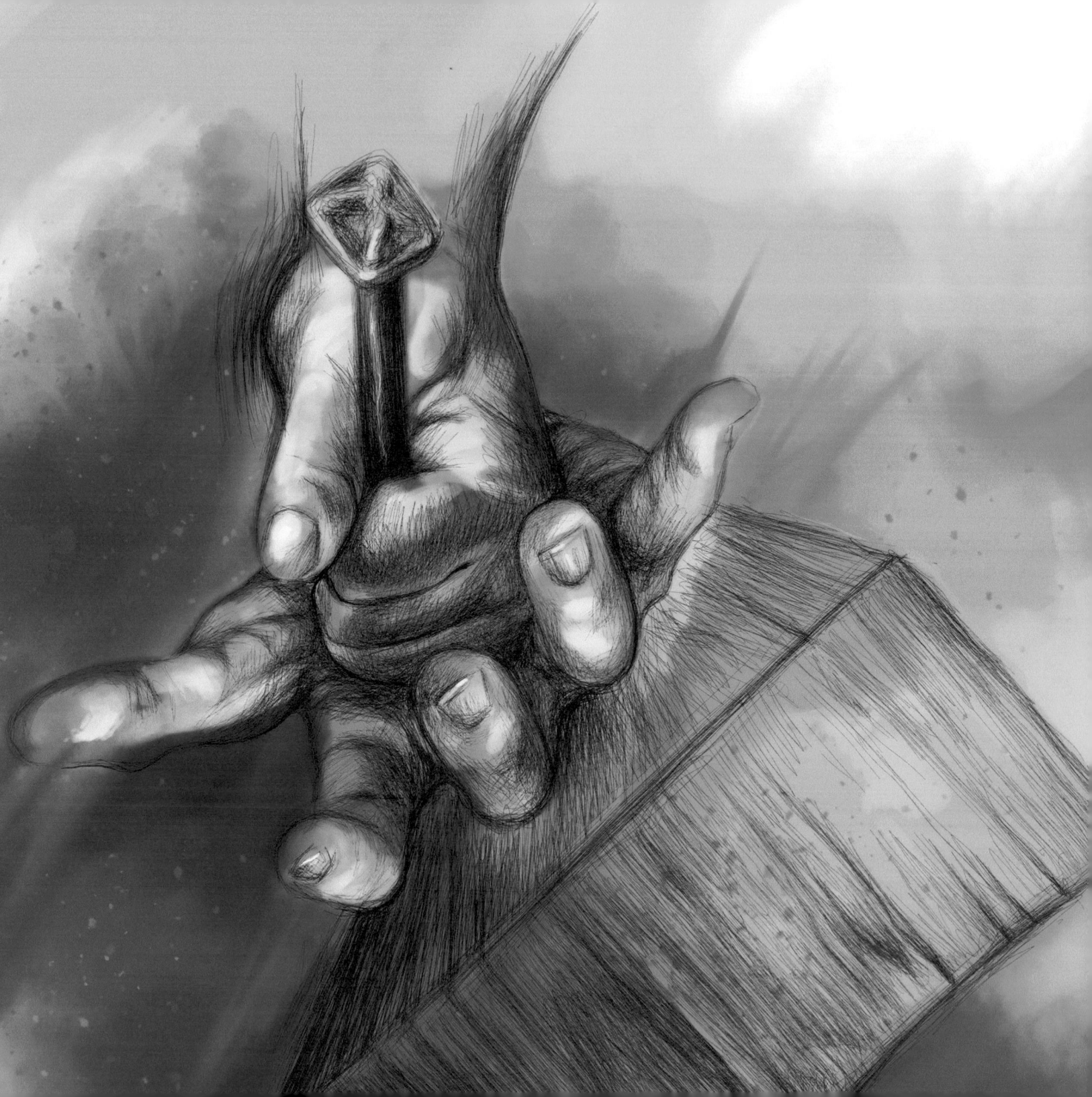

The Face of Love

Love is meek and is not puffed up. Many times it is submissiveness, being quiet and carefully listening while others speak, for love is polite. Love is strength, even when people mistake this attribute for weakness. Love is not selfish but is kind. It doesn't boast or brag, nor does it claim ownership of what is mine. Love is all about patience and sacrificing. Love is a gift. It was not given to bring down. It intentionally brings joy, for love simply uplifts. The Word tells us that it covers a multitude of our wrongs.

Christ laid down His life for every one of us, and He did it so that we could obtain eternal life. Salvation is trading in our old lives for new ones. There is renewed life to be found, but it is only in God's Son. Christ's love helps us shine brightly, and His blood covers our faults, enabling us to love one another God's way. His way is love past infinity, and that's definitely love without any limits. Loving our God first and then our neighbors is love that you cannot even begin to put a price on.

The way God loves His children is without conditions, for His love is unconditional. This love is given by the indwelling of God's Holy Spirit. Love is an action. We're supposed to display love with every breath of air we breathe. When we love God and others, we are humbled because the face of love is shown. Love is never gone. It grows stronger, lingers around and lasts forever.

Love never dies. It waits and then comes from within, for love abides. Love is never lost or done away with. It has been paid in full completely and our choice is whether or not to receive Christ's free gift of love. Love is loyal, hopeful and faithful. It doesn't give up but is temperate in all things, and is surely worth waiting for. Love is not unkind or cruel. Love doesn't block people, but is welcoming and overflowing like a flooded river—non-stop and constant. Love is not in darkness, and it is in true fellowship with the light.

Love is not forced but gentle. It restores without question. Love is giving to the poor not being greedy or having a heart that is always wanting more. Love is not staying stuck but getting up and making a difference, by moving, always doing something. Yes, love is an action. God's perfect love should always enable us to continually do right. Let us show God's face of love by loving everyone every day the way God tells us to.

Greater love hath no man than this, that a man lay down his life for his friends. — John 15:13

Introduction to Hate

Hate is not of God. In fact, it is contrary to His very characteristics. Hate goes against all of His standards, for God is love. When an individual says they hate you, they indeed are struggling with issues within themselves and are not in right relationship or standing with God our Father. We were made in His similitude and image, and His Word commands us to love Him and our neighbor without hesitation.

Hate causes bitterness, a stronghold that robs God's covenant people of the promises of His inheritance. Hate entraps us, allowing Satan, the enemy, to come in, causing separations and divisions. We are God's family, His people, His pasture, and our God is a God of unity. He created us all to love and to show love to one another daily.

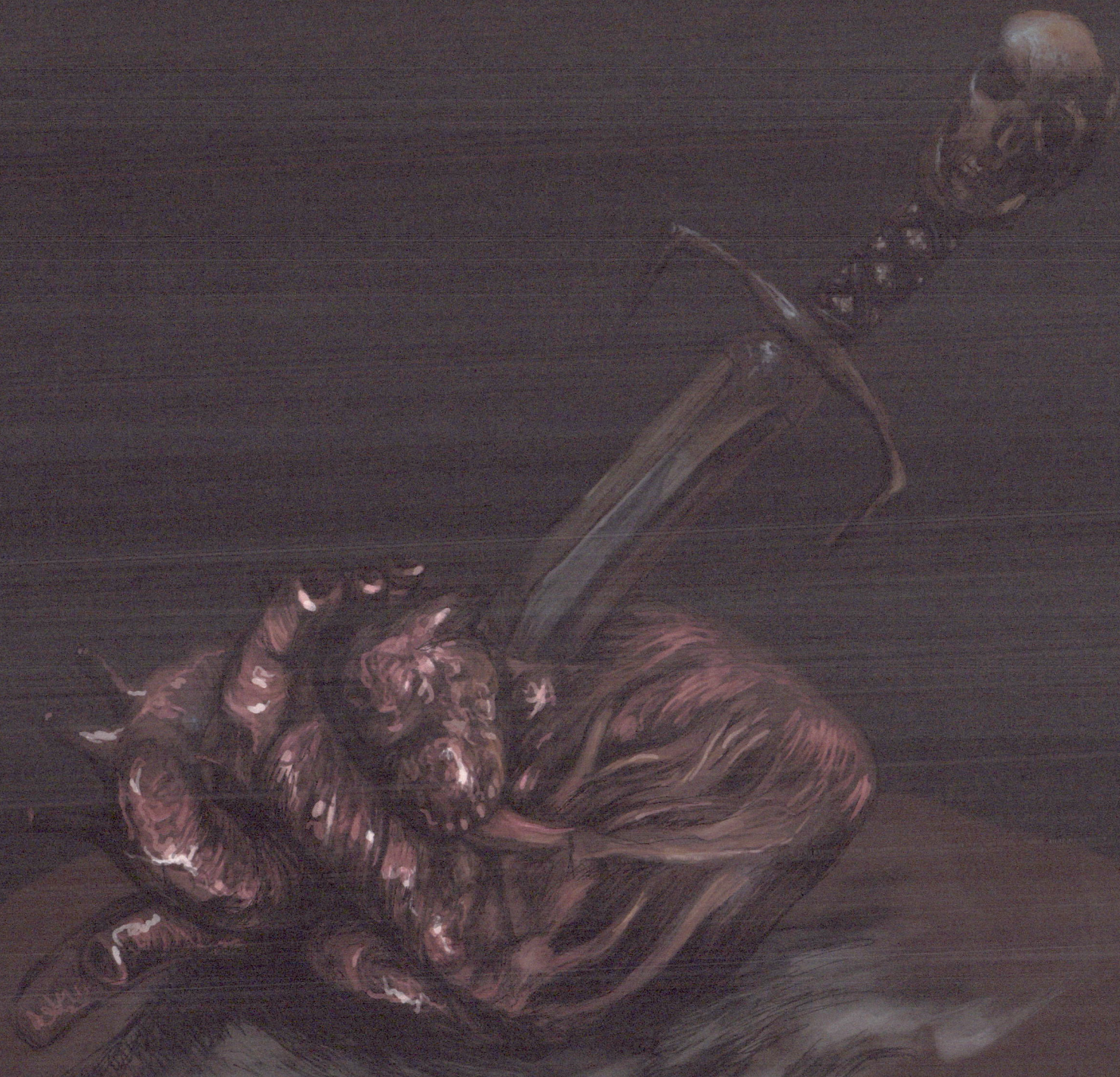

Hate

Hate is a very strong word that we, as believers, should never be classified or be associated with. Christ died and left us with His special gift of love, which overshadows all hate. Hate is very difficult because it doesn't agree with anyone.

Hate strips you and will have you mad and fighting everybody. "I hate you … because I'm not you," many say, when God gave each of us a chance to be renewed. Do you know what hate truly means?

Harboring
Attributes
Toward
Evil

Yes, My people, hate is a characteristic associated with Satan, the devil. Remember, his first mission hasn't changed. It is to steal, kill and destroy. Satan's ultimate mission is to kill a believer's joy. Hate will make you come up short and miss the mark, which is Heaven. Hate shouldn't even be mentioned in our vocabularies.

Hate can rob us of all God's promises. It's a heavy weight, not even worth carrying. God wants to give us a clean slate, because He is concerned about our entire state and wants to change our growth rate, simply because we're unable to save ourselves. If we try to do it alone, this will take us out of the safe state. Hate is, without question, a state of bondage. Love is, indeed, God's way of saving us, letting us get to know Him and canceling the enemy's plan.

Introduction to Shine

Many times we let our lights grow dim or even go out completely because of the circumstances we encounter in life. We cannot allow our situations to get the best of us and cause us to have an identity crisis. When this happens, we change who we are, whose we are and whom we believe in. We really need to know, without a shadow of a doubt, that God knows all about our situations. He knows how and even has the right time set to deliver us out of all tribulations. We need to truly incorporate into our spiritual minds the fact that we serve an amazing, omnipotent (all-powerful), omniscient (all-knowing) and omnipresent (everywhere at once) God, who is truly bigger than our problems.

God allowed these particular problems to exist for His glory, and we musts always remember that He has also created an expiration date for our trials. Our job is to trust Him and take Him at His Word. He is not like men (liars). First of all, He is perfect, holy and honest. If God said it, then it will be (see Numbers 23:19). In God's Word, His Holy Scriptures, we have what are called The Beatitudes. Some call them the Beautiful Attitudes. They teach us to let our light so shine before men that they may see our good works and glorify our Father which is in Heaven (see Matthew 5:16).

Let us be encouraged to let our lights shine so bright that we continue to focus on Christ and not our problems, remembering that He will never leave us nor forsake us. If He brought us to this moment, He will strengthen us and bring us through it. We have all encountered things in the past that we thought we could never make it through, but you're still breathing, and you still have Jesus. So, you've made it. It didn't feel good at the time, and some of our trials have left us with scars. But that's okay because scars are a indication or proof that we've weathered the storm and are still overcomers by our testimonies. Our trials, then, have made us stronger, and we can now talk about them, encouraging and telling someone else how we overcame and got the victory in Jesus. Thank You, Jesus! I'm broken but not bound (I didn't stay stuck). God has freed me from the chains of my past, and I will walk with my head held high into my future. I made it, and will continue to make it with God's help.

Shine

God gave us His Son, Jesus, and we see Him hanging, bleeding and dying on the cross, so that men could surrender all to Him. We are lights meant to shine so bright that we exceed the maximum capacity which is specified for each of our lamps. We must remember, when walking after Christ, our minds are transformed and renewed, so we must quickly forget this dying world's standards. Lamps, in reality, were not meant to hold us to begin with. In God we trust. Now where is *your* faith? Do you truly believe this?

God not only wants to shape but also perfect His people by molding us, yes, into vessels of honor. The Word enlightens us by making our vision sharper then any two-edged sword, and with God, there are no stops. We just praise Him and keep moving forward. Pleasing God is our priority and nothing else truly matters. I'm talking about getting distracted by the cares of this life. Let us shine now by not only studying, but also making it a top priority to adopt a prayer life. God wants us to seek His face. We somehow want others to run, but God wants *us* to turn it into a persistent chase after Him with all of our hearts.

Shine brightly, for we are walking epistles. Many people don't even open their Bibles for themselves. They look to others of God's people to be examples. Let us start today by sharing Jesus! He already gave us the victory by paving the way for every one of us. Please continue to reverence God's Son by keeping your end of the covenant in this blessed union—the true reason we live, move and have our being. This race called life was given, and we should fall on our knees and thank God for new mercies daily. Darkness wants to take over by choking off the very air we breathe. Our beliefs will open the keys to everlasting life, which adds up to an eternity. Greater is He who is within me. Shine so that everyone can see the Jesus in you. What are you waiting for?

Let your light so shine before men, that they may see your good works, and glorify your Father which is in heaven. — Matthew 5:16

Introduction to Stuck in Yesterday

Stuck—"immovable, attached, fixed." God has already sent us freedom (we all received this gift) and liberty, when He sent His only Son to die on that old rugged cross. The freedom is totally up to us. God has given us a choice, whether to stay free or continue in a state of bondage. When you're stuck, you're bound, not able to move, neither can you do the things you wish. You're in a fixed state. You have become attached to someone or something and need deliverance. God is the Deliverer and the only One who can deliver us out of being stuck. Many times we allow problems and situations to get the best of us instead of taking them to God, who is bigger and able to fix all of them and bring us out. There is no excuse.

Jesus didn't stay stuck. He got up, just like He said He would. *"And Jesus came and spake unto them, saying, All power is given unto me in heaven and in earth"* (Matthew 28:18). He was raised up with all power in His hands. But God has given His children that same power, not to stay stuck, but to get up. Therefore, even though you may be going through, God's Word is your power and is able to resurrect, rescue and resuscitate us by bringing us back to life. Isaiah recorded, *"But he was wounded for our transgressions; he was bruised for our iniquities: the chastisement of our peace was upon him; and with his stripes we are healed"* (Isaiah 53:5). Therefore, we are left without excuse. So, be quiet, dust yourself off and keep going.

In reading the Word of God, we can relate and reflect on the cities of Sodom and Gomorrah. Lot, Abraham's nephew, was living in the city of Sodom. God was getting ready to destroy that city, but He remembered Abraham and what he had asked for. Abraham found favor in God's sight, so because of Abraham, Lot and his family had a chance to escape. During their escape, they were warned not to look back upon the destruction that was going on. Then the Lord sent a rain of burning sulfur down from the sky onto Sodom and Gomorrah and destroyed those wicked cities. He also destroyed the whole Jordan Valley, everyone living in the two cities and even all the plant and animal life.

As we know, Lot's wife looked back, and when she did, she was turned into a pillar of salt (see Genesis 19:24-26). The key verse is 26, where Lot's wife looked back and lost her life. God was delivering them from their yesterdays and the state of bondage in the city of Sodom, but this women was stuck in her past and couldn't let go by trusting God and taking Him at His Word. The result was that she became her past, her yesterday. She was stuck in the very destruction the Deliverer was trying to deliver her out of, and her yesterday consumed her. God has freed us from being stuck in our yesterdays and healed us from the brokenness and pains of our past. He has renewed us and set us free from the old way of thinking.

If the Son therefore shall make you free, ye shall be free indeed. — John 8:36

Stuck in Yesterday

I was stuck in yesterday, but yesterday truly brought me a lot of pain. I thought all of my problems got washed away, right along with the enraged winds and torrent of rains. But yesterday was valuable. It taught me that I should never aim to please the people on this earth, also known as man. I was reminded that my true Father abides in the clouds above, and He is the Creator of everything, also known to us as the GREAT I AM.

I was stuck in yesterday, for I was ashamed of the things I did, yes, awful things that wouldn't even let me be considered as a child of the King. Yesterday I had an argument with one of my brethren. Oh, it wasn't the things I said that condemned me, but the terrible things I turned around and did. These were things that wouldn't even allow me to be considered Kingdom fit.

If someone wrongs you, don't turn around and hurt them back. "An eye for an eye" was the old way. Seek the Scriptures for yourself. Christ freed us from that bondage way of living. The Word of God is all truth, nothing but pure facts. I was stuck in yesterday because I thought all hope was lost and I was through … until I repented to the living God. He said, "I wasn't finished making you." God not only forgives us; He is the God of second chances.

I was stuck in yesterday because I had a problem looking unto man. I've broken the Golden Rules, which are the first and second commandments. God is the One to whom all of my faith, hope and love belongs. If you don't treat your neighbor right, He will disown and dismiss you out of His sight. I was stuck in yesterday, but yesterday made me stronger. It taught me not to give up so fast and to stick it out by hanging in there a little longer. Yesterday truly helped me to discover who I was. If you name the name of Christ, you will have troubles and struggles. Oh, and you're not somehow exempt from sinning. But if we admit our faults, He is just to forgive them. And it is His blood that cleanses us from all unrighteousness.

I was stuck in yesterday, but God reminded me to turn the page, for He'd already forgiven me. He told that there were new mercies for the new day and that I could be better today than yesterday. "Forget yesterday," He said. "It's gone, and now it's considered your past. Remember, start today off with prayer, My Word and your very best praise. Yesterday wasn't meant to hurt you, but it brought you purpose and much success because the pain you experienced aided in your spiritual growth for today." So, don't look back to your past. God has already delivered you from Egypt.

Introduction to Fishermen

God wants us to go into the world and teach non-believers about Him by sharing the Gospel with them. When Christ called the disciples, they were from different backgrounds. They left all they had to follow Him. God has no respect of persons; He wants to use every one of us for His glory. He wants all men to be saved, and it is our job to go out into the world and begat other disciples. We fish for people by adhering to God's words, applying and sharing what we've learned with unbelievers, the ones who don't have a relationship with Him. Let us go into the world and do what Christ has instructed us to do.

Fishermen

Jesus told us to go into the world and be fisher's of men. What did you think He was talking about when He told us to teach all nations about Him, the Author and Finisher of our faith? We have been impatient and keep picking and choosing which words we will obey and wondering why we keep losing our bait. God is telling us not to lose focus, but to be still and know that He is God. We must also continue to trust Him. "Child," He is saying, "where is your faith? Walk after Me and get rid of old habits that keep getting your net stuck and entangled with presumptuous sins and worthless stuff. If the methods you've chosen to fish with just don't seem to be working, get back in the boat, stop getting distracted, and stop trying to do it on your own. Use the methods and instructions that I've chosen for you to fish with. If you do, the fish will surely bite.

"You begin to hesitate because your flesh kicks in, and you're feeling tired, so you feel like it's pointless to keep trying because you have labored and labored and haven't caught a thing all night. Hold on! Don't let up just yet! The catch will come in My timing, which is perfect, and not yours. Now, at My command, cast your nets once again, trusting Me with all of your heart and stop all the doubting. Lower your nets, for the harvest is plentiful and the laborers are few. I've called you to be fishers of men in a world filled with nothing but sin. Yes, this fishing expedition is spiritual, and the fish you're catching are souls for My Kingdom. Let down your nets. It's time for the big catch."

And he saith unto them, Follow me, and I will make you fishers of men. — Matthew 4:19

Then saith he unto his disciples, The harvest truly is plenteous, but the laborers are few. — Matthew 9:37

Introduction to Depression, Depression

I am an overcomer of depression. It was my God and much prayer going out on my behalf that kept me through it. I wanted to stay in the house, secluded. I lost a lot of weight. It was a terrible time. The devil played with my mind, and I wanted to end my life. It was only a trap to hinder me from doing what God had called me to do. I thank Him for delivering me from the bondage of depression.

The mind is our main battleground, and we, as believers, need to protect our minds. If someone has your mind, then they have the best part of you. They are able to manipulate and control you. They will have you do everything they want you to do. You will not be able to think and make decisions on your own.

The spirit of control is of the devil. The only One who is totally in control of all things is God. We need Him to arrest our minds, for there are so many things trying to get our attention. God wants us to be in a state of peace. When we are in a state of peace, we can be totally focused on His will for our lives. Depression is of the enemy and is definitely a state of bondage. I'm here to let you know to be encouraged. If I overcame it, so can you—only with God.

Depression, Depression

Oh, where have you come from?

Just another trick of the enemy

To keep believers distracted, cast down with no joy.

I speak victory because God says I've already won.

He told me to speak over my situation because life and death are in the power of the tongue.

I am an overcomer by the blood of the Lamb and the words of my testimony.

Therefore, depression has no place here.

God says, "My dear, think pure thoughts of peace and not of evil.

Do not be discouraged or intimidated by that old devil.

Speak peace and tell him to flee, for I've conquered these trials also in the flesh.

The agony and sweat like drops of blood were truly signs of stress.

Depression came in when I asked My Father to let this cup pass from Me.

Nevertheless, I stayed there, endured and died, so that your sins could be erased.

Remember, whom the Son sets free is free indeed.

Please be transformed by the renewing of your mind.

No more distractions!

I need you to be Kingdom minded.

Keep trusting and be freed, My child,

For I am calling you to be in a state of perfect peace."

Thou wilt keep him in perfect peace, whose mind is stayed on thee: because he trusteth in thee. — Isaiah 26:3

Introduction to Hold On to Your Faith

This faith poem was written to encourage God's people not to give up. Faith is nothing new. It is our oxygen to survive spiritually, for without it we are considered dead. It's like the flow of blood through our bodies. Without it, the body cannot operate or function properly.

Many times, in our walk with God, our faith is tried and tested, to see whether we have what it takes to weather the storm. The Word of God tells us that *"without faith it is impossible to please God, for He that cometh to God must believe that he is, and that he is a rewarder of them that diligently seek him"* (Hebrews 11:6). Our faith is vital and dictates our relationship with our heavenly Father. God indeed wants a relationship with all His children, but the decision is left totally up to each of us. He has given us the alternative—to believe and have a life of peace or not to believe and be tormented forever.

Hold On to Your Faith

Faith is the substance of things hoped for and the evidence of things not seen. Faith is narrowed down to our trust and courage to just believe. Faith is counting it done, although it may seem that the battle is still raging. Faith is the power of knowing that the race is already won—even before your foot is set to the runner's mark. Faith is trusting God's navigation when you don't have a map, a clue or compass nor any idea as to where you're going. Faith is believing that you're already healed, when you just received bad news from your doctor.

Faith is trusting that you will receive that new job, when you just received a pink slip stating that your services are no longer needed and you're not qualified to be hired by anyone else. Faith is getting that new house when the bank called you a couple of days ago and told you that you were not approved. Faith is continuing the race set before you, even though you may feel that you don't have enough strength to finish. Faith is the power of pushing, with God-given endurance, our hopes placed in Christ. We are indeed always on the winning side.

Faith the size of a mustard seed is what our cloud of witnesses before us believed God for, and God fulfilled their promises. Faith is having confidence, although it may seem that what you're praying or hoping for is just too impossible. Faith is trusting God to bring to pass the things hidden right before your eyes. Keep watching, praying and believing, and He will reveal it—only in His time. Hold on to His words and take them with you everywhere you go. God says that faith is not seen with the natural eye. It is spiritual. Faith is trusting Him with all our hearts.

Let us stop holding on to fear and trust God to fulfill His every word (see Hebrews 11:1 and 12:1).

Introduction to the Righteous Path

There are two paths in life, and it's truly up to us which one of them we decide to follow. There is a righteous path and an unrighteous road that we can choose. There are a couple of things you need to know about these two choices. Only one of them can be chosen, each of them will get you to a sure destination, and you cannot travel both at the same time. The choice is left completely up to each individual and will determine their final destination.

These two choices have distinct and sure consequences. The unrighteous road is big, busy and popular. It is taken frequently, but choosing to take this unrighteous road will cause you many heartaches and many sorrows, and, in the end, it will lead you to destruction and death. Although the righteous path is the one that is unpopular and less traveled, it is the one that will bring you joy, peace and eternal life. Therefore, we should make it our business to choose this path every time.

You may have noticed that I called one a *path* and the other a *road*. A path is one already laid out (salvation is only found in Jesus Christ). Our Savior already paved this way for believers to take. He said in His Word, *"I am the way, the truth, and the life: no man cometh unto the Father, but by me"* (John 14:6).

The Righteous Path

I will not walk, stand or sit on the corrupt road. Corrupt behavior is like germs, spreading quickly like a virus considered contagious, deadly and sin-sick. If not treated properly, you're on the road to death and destruction. The cure is salvation, only found in God's Son, Jesus. Bright lights must stay lit. Fellowshipping with the darkness makes us ungodly, displaying bad characteristics, which make us like the Pharisees. Their standards were not godly but found only within themselves. The Savior described them as hypocrites, and in His Word that kind of religion is described as useless.

Tradition is also known to make an individual self-righteous and unfit for God's Kingdom. Who did you think the words in the Holy Scriptures were written for? Did you think they were without meaning or value, of no worth? The righteous may fall seven times but rises up and stands tall in the sight of God. The righteous are like trees planted by overflowing rivers of waters. Sinners are not recognized and will not stand among the just, because they're not concerned about the things of God. In His sight, they are not only cut off; but unbelievers are considered abandoned and classified as lost, for they fail to obey the words of the living God.

The ungodly are already dead because they have rejected the ways of Christ's cross. Even though no man has an excuse, God gave each one a choice. Everyone shakes their heads and gives nods, but who will truly go hard and take a stand for God. You may be frightened because your so-called friends classify you as not fitting in or odd. Choose God today over this perishing world. Salvation is the key. God will abundantly pardon your sins, and He is waiting to deliver you. Let go and let God do a new thing in you. You need to stop "putting on" and really believe God for your freedom.

Enter through the narrow gate. For wide is the gate and broad is the road that leads to destruction, and many enter through it. — Matthew 7:13, NIV

Introduction to I Will Go, Lord

Many times, as believers, we get nervous and become afraid. Immediately we begin to question the calling that the Lord has on our lives. God is telling us to be confident and know that we are His. When He calls us, He gives us clear instructions as to what He is calling us to do. He wants us to be assured that He has us and will guide us through the entire journey.

Many times, on the journey, we feel that we are not equipped or qualified and don't have what it takes to get the job done. God has already equipped us and prepared us for the assignment at hand. There are times when we travel alone, but we are not alone, for God is with us every step of the way. He just wants us to accept the call He has on our lives. He is looking for willing vessels to work for His Kingdom. Our answer to the call of God should always be "YES!" It may take some of us longer than others, but we should always be ready and available for God's work, so that He can get all of the glory out of our lives.

I Will Go, Lord

I will go, Lord. Please send me. But first I need You to cleanse me of all sins, unrighteousness. Father, don't forget to refill me with Your precious Spirit. I need it to fulfill the missions You are sending me on, without delay or distractions. Please hear my humble prayer, petitions and pleas. I will go, Lord. I'm a little nervous. Is it all right for your warrior to ask for more strength and courage?

"It's okay!" God says. "My dear, there is no fear. Just keep seeking and watching, and remember: I'll never leave nor forsake you. I'll do the same for you as I did in the days of my servant Joshua. Remember, I am the Lord your God, and I change not."

I will go, Lord, not knowing that the battles on this journey are mostly fought alone.

"Others cannot go with you. You are in a promotion process, so stop looking back. I purposely destroyed so-called friendships so that your focus would be directly on Me. The shift didn't feel good, but it was necessary so that you could rightfully take your place. I knew what I was doing when I chose you and deemed you qualified. I must tell you the truth, my child. I cannot lie. The road ahead is rough, and there are trying times ahead. But don't get discouraged. Stay in the Word and remember, hang in there. Don't faint. And one more thing: you mustn't forget to pray."

I will go, Lord.

"Although it seems that many doors were closed in your face, there was a reason, and it was not to discourage you. If you had gone through them, you would have abused the opportunities, forgotten the assignment completely and all of the reasons as to why I was sending you."

I will go, Lord. I'm ready to fulfill my duties. Lord, I am available, and my answer, without question, is "Yes!"

God says, "I've already given you courage, so please continue to press, for this is indeed an open-book test."

God fights for His warriors, and they always win the war by finishing strong. He has already given us the victory.

Also I heard the voice of the LORD, saying, whom shall I send, and who will go for us? Then said I, Here am I; send me. — Isaiah 6:8

All Things

Jesus said, "*All things are possible to him that believes.*" Who dares stand in question of the living God, who does all things well? Jesus walked on water, spoke peace to the raging seas and calmed storms. At His command, even the winds behaved. He cleansed the lepers, healed all manner of disease and even called Lazarus to come forth from the grave that held him. God of all things, Jesus was born fully human and completely divine. He took upon Himself flesh, but still He did not know any sort of sin. He rose from the grave on the third day, with all power in His hands. God of all things, He turned around and questioned death, asking, "*Where is thy sting?*" He declared total victory, and He is the God who still reigns.

The heavens and the earth belong to Him and the fullness thereof. The only thing hindering us is unbelief, doubt or a lack of trust. God said that all things are possible with Him and simply impossible without Him. You must believe that He is and that He will reward you without hesitation if you constantly seek His face, withholding nothing, if you delight yourself in His presence. Our God is the Source of all things, and nothing is able to function and operate without Him.

All things are possible with God, and without Him things become impossible. They break down and just fall apart. Therefore, men are encouraged to turn away from their sins and seek Him diligently with their whole heart. All things were created and made for His glory and purpose, but we get purpose twisted when our main jobs as servants are to worship Him and offer up our service. We must show everyone that the love of God shines within. We have somehow lost our focus.

I'm not talking about a traditional church. This is service outside of the four walls, taking the Gospel to the streets. Yes, the unconditional love of God is *agape*.

God said that He created man in His image, but we refuse to present our bodies daily as sacrifices. He is holding us to a higher accountability. How dare we hide our lights and disobey by refusing to unseal our lips and offer up the best praises. Instead, we fold our arms, stomp our feet, close our hearts and let our emotions take over, making the choice to let the flesh rule and continuously disobey Him. He created men and gave them a choice to follow Him or not.

God ordained men, chose them, called them, and unselfishly gave them gifts. He said that all things were good that He had made, and He did it all by Himself. It was the work of His mighty hands. He is the King of kings and with him nothing is lost, but, rather, found, restored, refilled, refreshed and made new!

All things belong to Him—even the day for its doom. All things are possible, and there is nothing too hard that He is not able to simply do. But it is all according to His plan and our faith.

Stop all of the complaining and doubting. He's just waiting to fulfill all things, yes, all of His promises, all the things He has said concerning you.

If thou canst believe, all things are possible to him that believeth. — Mark 9:23

Release Me

Release me, God, from all of my past pains. I was so busy focusing on what I had lost that I could hardly see the new season that came in, nor the blessings You gave. Release me from the brokenness of relationships, from the skeletons of never being good enough, never making it my business to fit in with the so-called friends, nor the circles that surrounded me. Release me from the down talk of people who are saying, "You're a disappointment! You'll never be anything or measure up to much!"

Release me from the brokenness within my marriage, the sleepless nights, the worthless quarrels, the nonverbal fights, issues that continue to torture me, punishments from my past. Release me from anything and everything that hinders or threatens a well-pleasing relationship with You. Release me from church people who are too busy judging me according to their fleshly standards, by questioning my salvation, to see if God really called or chose me. God told me to release it by giving it all to Him, and when I did, it didn't matter anymore.

God says, "These were mountains in your life which you already received the power to speak to and remove. You survived to tell the story. You overcame the storm, and this is your testimony, for you now have the scars to prove it. Keep trusting in Me, child. Your pain and suffering wasn't for naught. It was all for My glory."

I would like to thank God again for all He has done for me, bringing me out of seventeen years of bondage. No more chains, for He has set me free and delivered me. God said that the curse is lifted, so I will continue to praise Him and give Him all of the glory forever.

Once again, I would like to thank everyone who had a part in making this book a reality. Be encouraged in the Lord, and be blessed through the ministry of poems that bring healing. Let God heal and deliver you today. God loves you, and so do I.

Michelle Stadard

No Fear

" Be Strong And Courageous... "

Joshua 1:9

www.ingramcontent.com/pod-product-compliance
Lightning Source LLC
LaVergne TN
LVHW070909080426

835513LV00004B/116